YES

a youthful election system

yes

a youthful election system

voting = articulation of people

ISBN ~ 978-1-291-69598-4
February 14th, 2014 ~ Apprenti

Creator ~ Maestro S'ace de Groot
Author ~ Prof. PhD Wil'fred Bastiani

Epitome

This book is a summary of the Dutch book "*Een **J**eugdig **K**ies**S**ysteem*", literally translated into the English language. The book was written in February 2011 based upon the thinking of S'ace de Groot. The idea for a new election system emerged out of a competition entry which entailed writing an essay for the Dutch daily newspaper "***N**ew **R**otterdam's **C**ourant*" - the NRC. The title of the competition in 1990 was "*Is everything said that needs to be said?*". It was based upon the frustrations evoked by the current political governments at the time.

A "***Y**outhful **E**lection **S**ystem ~ YES*" is the improvement of dynamics within election processes and is organic and systemic. The question is whether an election system currently presented with adult bias is still appropriate. When is someone really an adult and does it really have to do with the numerical value of age? I will explain the association of the words "*electing*" and "*youthful*" later in this book. Secondly it is about the static aspect within a "*1 vote system*" that implies that the voter would prefer to vote for only 1 person to be his or her representative within politics. It is comparable to having 1 Euro with the possibility only to be permitted to buy bread with it. Mankind needs a diversity of food to be able to live in a healthy way.

A "*Youthful Election System*" complies with this diversity principle because each voter has a number of points to designate between possible political representatives who appeal to his or her (ethical) principles. One can ask whether having 20 Euros instead of 1 Euro would affect the results of shopping in a supermarket and what choices one would make and why. Surely this is as personal as it can be, being based upon logic or values or perhaps even a combination of multiple aspects. A third and static aspect is the election cycle of 4 years. During the period of 4 years, essential changes occur which may require new ways for governments and different political instigators. Its static character is its considerable disadvantage and is expressed by the slow and sluggish decision processes of huge institutions unless personal interests are at stake.

In a way the principles of YES are applicable for any system or institution that applies elections within their selection for "*the "right person at the right position*" ~ in relationship to one's qualities and capabilities. Why are CEO´s appointed by boardrooms without consulting any employer of the company itself ? Who really takes care of the production and thus affirms with these activities the functionality ~ the right of existence ~ of the organization ? Who in fact is acting and who is facilitating during these processes ?

However nowadays it about the right integrity. To me integrity is some equivalence of intelligence. I ever heard a slogan of some CEO : "*I am not intelligent, but I am sociable.*" It indicates that this CEO hasn't got a clue that intelligence has to deal with all facets in life, whether it is about logics, values, sociability, physical and psychical skills and even more aspects. How can such a CEO make decisions that are strongly coherent ? Intelligence is an integrality; it implies an inner actualization of all required potential and dimensional intelligences together manifested into the outer world, represented as an integer behaviour by its "*owner*" ~ "*walk the talk*".

Politicians, C?O's and members of the boardrooms of multinationals are incriminated of personal interests that often is hard to prove because of the closed character of firstly the selection system and secondly the communication and thirdly the influence of money that determines the choices made by politicians. Most are not capable to deal with our so called reality in a pragmatic and integral way. The connection between logics and values is disturbed or isn't even often accomplished. Theoreticians that tell how life should be lived, how work should be done without any true experience and evaluating themselves.

If you read this in the right way you may notice that is about the "*how*". How is the technocratic way of realizing or accomplishing "*something*". What really goes beyond this something they can't tell. How is the easy world of solutions, the 1 dimensionality of issues, the short time success story while ignoring integrality and thus disrespecting sustainability.

When their crimes and~or indiscretions are revealed publically nothing happens often. The show must go on and the next C?O or minister stands up to take over the control within the same conditions, even dodgier than his or her predecessor. That's what matters, the voter has no influence anymore during these 4 years when agreements are broken and promises are not fulfilled. Any political party can introduce their own representative persons after the elections that it thinks of they are capable to do the job. Controlled by the conditions and demarcations of that same political party.

This epitome represents a summarized superficial description of YES. It may also become a personal study book, it depends how you deal with this information; in a single- or a pluri-dimensional way. Intelligence is about all dimensions, its associations and its potentials to actualize these afterwards. So this book and its information have more implicated dimensions that present the uniqueness of this new system.

Let's find out, have fun reading it.

A Youthful Election System

Introduction

Anywhere we look around in the formal structures election systems are based upon 1 vote per participant. In the meanwhile there exist playful systems where election systems are based upon values and figures. Why isn't that possible for our Government ?

Since Rudolph Thorbecke introduced this kind of election system about 150 years ago nothing has changed ever. The election period of 4 years have remained the same. Some new aspects were the voting rights for women and the age of 18 for voting ~ voter ~ and 21 for being voted ~ the candidate. Besides this we know several election systems, firstly in this book we deal with the local and the national elections every 4 years.

Points

The election system YES is based upon points instead of 1 vote every time. YES starts at the moment of the age of 16 years for local elections, 18 years for the national elections and 21 years for being a candidate for both.

The essence is that at the moment one gets 16, 18 or 21 years (s)he doesn't have to wait until the actual moment of elections. In the worst case someone should be waiting 4 years minus 1 day. At the moment of one's birthday of 16 (s)he becomes 20 points to be spent for local elections. At the moment of one's birthday of 18 (s)he becomes 20 points to be spent for national elections.

After 7 years this individual becomes 20 more points to spend, so when (s)he is 23 years old (s)he may spend 40 point for the local elections and at the age of 25 (s)he has 40 point for the national elections and so on. What is the difference between 1 vote and points ? In the epitome I described the example of the budget in the supermarket. Having points implies the possibility to choose more representatives and the more the issue is that this representative deals with the more points you will grant. In a table it looks like next.

Age		Type	
16	20 points	local	Individual development by accepting Positive disintegration
18	20 points	national	
23	40 points	local	
25	40 points	national	
30	60 points	local	
32	60 points	national	
37	80 points	local	
39	80 points	national	
44	100 points	local	Stabilization
46	100 points	national	
51	80 points	local	Collective development by sharing Negative disintegration
53	80 points	national	
58	60 points	local	
60	60 points	national	
65	40 points	local	
67	40 points	national	
72	20 points	local	
74	20 points	national	

Of course it is very interesting who will get the points and how its deviation will be. Every variation is characterized by the individual who does the voting and dividing of the points. The character of the results by the point division for each representative is congruent to the character of a mental sane and intelligent individual. Each representative is a duplicate of the voter concerning inspiration, ideas, ambitions and ethics.

If we imagine the table as a diagram it represents some pyramid with its top around the age of 42-49 years. This period in one's life implies the point of pivotation. One is capable to discuss open minded and it willing to transduce the experience to the next generation. The benefits out of the society that guaranteed one's development and intelligent disintegration during the posterior years will be made available to the Newbies.
An example :

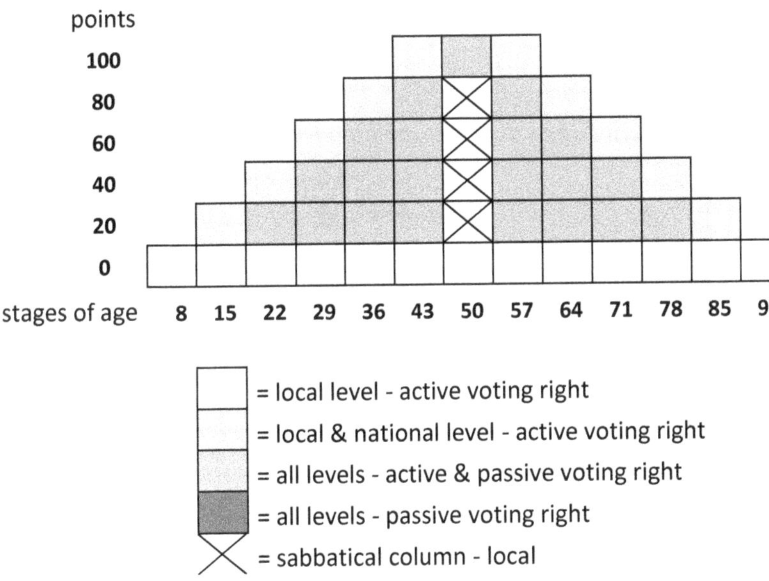

If we want to play a new game there are new rules, as few as possible because rules and demarcations kill creativity and its dynamics. However we made the next suggestions. Of course they can be discussed and changed.

- As a starting point we choose 20 points to divide
- The starting age is one's birthday of 16 at local level
- Maximally half the amount of all points may be given to 1 candidate
- Maximally 11 candidates can be selected like a soccer team

- Every 7 years the amount of points will be raised with 20 points
- All points are to be divided

In the middle there is the possibility for candidates to take a sabbatical year or period to make up one's mind for the coming years.

Another innovative aspect is that a potential candidate doesn't need to be a member of a political party; (s)he may be neutral. Candidates are selected by their skills, experiences and wisdom. Relevant candidates introduce themselves for the coming election within some theme or discipline. It is even better that there exist no political parties at all. Most debates between different politicians end up in more polarity than before, because the principles of each political party need to be respected whether they serve the issue or not.

Discrimination of age

While introducing and explaining this new election system to friends of ours the most often mentioned issue we heard is the discrimination of age after the age of 50 ~ see the table. While man grows older ~ around 45 years ~ the number of points diminish. That sounds illogical because "*wisdom increases by life experience*" ~ normally speaking. However these wiser individuals become less points to divide and so have less power to influent the results of elections.

In that point of view it is right. However it is about a generation transcending society; a variety of individuals including their ages. This implies that the knowledge and skills of older generations may not overrule or even block the innovation of the new generation. What is important here is that the cultural and moral values beyond any innovation will be respected. The issue of any living being is to develop itself at the benefit of the society. During these years man has the opportunity to establish the society in accordance with one's own values.

As Socrates ever said about a democracy : "*The right governor dares to be governed.*" It implies that the learning years are at the benefit for the individual and at the benefit of the society afterwards. If man decides to make wrong or egoistic decisions or choose corrupt governors into politics, then later on (s)he has to deal with the effects of those decisions that are hard to correct afterwards because the number of points have diminished. So the diminishing of points is some guarantee for continuity of high qualitative life for everyone at every moment for all days.

It is important that children are raised well, respectful and sociable; they are the future of our own benefits and they have the opportunity to influent maximally because of their high amount of points. Every ethical failure during their youthful years will be a punishment or disrespect for the parents or peers who were responsible for it then.

A premature participating involvement in an electoral system the way YES represents may contribute to a better identifying and defining their own self and their talents to finally become emotional-stabilized civilians. YES offers the opportunity to learn taking responsibility from the age of 16 during local elections to experience it in a playful manner to get used to such processes.

Denying or ignoring to educate the youthful individuals in a moral way will lead to an egoistic society at the moment they get positioned at important functions and deal with power and control. So during your own life you have the opportunities to raise your children right, respect the social minors and take care of a well-balanced society. That is the mission, that is the unheard silence within a generation binding system like YES, the so-called "*Generation Binding S'ilence*".

Another part of the mission is openness. If we want an open and transparent society why does everybody do so mysteriously about the choice they made during election time ? YES pursues publicly and openly voting by everyone, the candidates being the examples. It is quite strange that our representatives act that way; presenting the opposite way of this openness and transparency. Closed moralities like that avoid any kind of dialogue in advance. The dialogue in advance that guarantees an open and healthy democracy the way we want a democracy to be, not afterwards. Openness is the start for integrity.

Way of voting

With our daily technology it is possible to do the voting in other ways than the paper versions. It is possible to create and develop a Vote-Apps that replaces the old fashion way of voting.

First of all it is important to realize that voting isn't an isolated moment of choosing representatives or a political party. It is about the process. How many politicians really "*Walk their Talk*" ? How many don't or are forced to do not by the system they land in ? It is strange that after the elections have passed new politicians are introduced by parties that are completely unknown to lots of people. What are their merits ? What are they capable to ?

So voting implies more than analysing the political field 2 weeks before the election date. Consciousness in life is an aspect that is important every day. So making an integer decision for selecting potential candidates you need to be in that process during the months and years between the successive election dates.

Let's summarize.

- With an app on your e.g. smart phone you can fill in your preferred candidates and assign each of them points for that moment and any other moment you like
- Through this app your voting history can show you your own selecting behavings and changes during a chosen period by using its memory and stored data

- Smart phones can be used to vote for candidates based upon your ID when elections are actual, other digital devices that properly equipped as well
- During the political period is possible to reveal that some politicians are no longer qualified and need to be exchanged by capable individuals. An in advance agreed percentage of responses may force that it really happens. It is like some referendum
- International or urgent and insistent issues can be discussed by sharing options to all people so they can vote for strategies and solutions. Best results can be debated by politicians before making single political decisions that haven't been approved and supported well by the majority of the inhabitants

In the current technological society it is a piece of cake to create such a device and-or app. Why doesn't it happen and do we remain in the ancient times of voting on paper ?

David van Reybrouck

David van Reybrouck is a Belgian author and invented the idea of gambling over new candidates. The inhabitants of Athens used to do so in the very past. It has an important advantage.

It isn't so that anyone can be selected to participate. It is about preselected reliable candidates that can be chosen by chance or tossing dice. The most important advantage is that it is almost impossible to make mutual agreements based upon selfish interests as it happens nowadays all the time. If potential candidates are intelligent, capable, integer and reliable then it doesn't matter who is to be chosen. It is about the content instead of the person.

The funniest part in his story when he presented it on television in 2013 was the fact that his idea can be combined with YES. The preliminary phase for selecting potential candidates can be accomplished through YES the final part by dice.

However YES knows an analogue process in the final compositions of governments. It is almost equal to the first stage. After the selected candidates are announced the possibility exists to vote for certain teams in the government. Nowadays in Holland we know the formators appointed by the queen or king who are responsible to create a team of ministers based upon results of an election. It concerns the division of the numbers of votes for each party totally.

See yourself as the main coach of a match and compose your strongest team as you think it has the ability be most successful to deal with issues. Therefore the same app can be used to reveal your preferences. That is what we call dynamic elections. While it takes lots of time and efforts before elections are prepared and people really can vote the current technology ~ when rightly developed and well-equipped ~ can introduce elections at any time. Preparations are minimal and every voter knows what to do and how to vote especially when youthful people are allowed tc participate in a responsible and playful circumstances. Tossing dice may be such a playful method that appeals to the newer generation.

The election process is dynamic and remains dynamic in that way. Elections have become about exchanging candidates for new ones without worrying about the so-called left, right, conservative, liberal or socio-liberal directions within the politics with all their fragmented interests and principles.

Epilogue

This book described a new election system. The essence of the addition "*youthful*" implies that this process of election is equivalent to the process of awareness and even consciousness, the everlasting learning process of (wo-)mankind during his or her life.

This election system offers each individual to develop and explicate one's own talents and insert these visions and intellect into the election process. If you ask someone its favourite food then you'll hear also a variety of products,. That is life. Most individuals who are asked to announce the favourite candidates for the government, would like to mention more than 1 preferred name. Often these names are related to different political parties and that is often the association to that mentioned candidate.

In essence you may recognize that it is not only the candidate itself, more it is his or her potential in relationship to the theme or issue. Why do we ~ even in 2014 ~ block the wishes for a broader possibility choosing more than 1 candidate ? Is that exactly that politics make abominable and disgusting ? The closed morality of govern a nation without truly hearing what the inhabitants want and why the politicians were chosen after all ? Acting in a selfish way where decisions are made based upon facts & figures and where human values are primarily neglected unless there is some space to deal with it ?

The democratic decision system has become a static and solid system that empowers itself because it doesn't allow any form of dynamics, per 4 years it allows some interchange with the outer world. The allowed influence by civilians don't go beyond the elections each 4 years. And when political parties appear to be unable to cooperate, to co-create that what is essential regarding the issue then they simply stop the process.

Personal interests and those of the political parties are more important than to find the right answers. Politics don't know the words "*synthesis & synergy*" anymore. Co-creation emerges out of these 2 aspects.

In dialogues it is about the ternary "*what/who*", the "*why*" and the "*how*" successively corresponding with Grammar, Dialogue and Rhetoric. In grammar we find the essence, its functionality whether we deal with a phenomenon or an issue or problem. Each essence has a specific intrinsic strength no matter who or how many people are involved. It also demands its own kind of action. These 3 aspects ~ "*essence-strength-action*" ~ are integral and need to be considered that way. They rely on "*the Laws of Nature*". It is up to us to get aware of them.

How many politicians don't deal with issues in this way ? How many times all debates are focused on "*how*" ? The question how a solution should be effective without truly knowing its essence and strength. This is solution-thinking acting in a 1-or 2-dimensional context; the linear cause-effect method. Besides that nowadays the Performance Indicator is most of the times money. Money as the metaphor and final consideration criterion for each issue. However it is about integrality and includes all dimensions.

It is easy to understand that afterwards human values get pinched. Lots of human values are related to natural laws. So it is peculiar that especially these values are primarily ignored, that earthly laws, rules and control are given preference above the rules of human values. The Performance Indicator "*Money*" kills any open dialogue about this, so does any law or rule being applied as arguments. It keeps any openness for a healthy dialogues away.

To find out about this ternary we added a game in this book. Try to find out what your preferences are concerning essence, strength and action. Knowing yourself better implies the opportunity to make a better decision for the next elections and have the right individuals represent you in the government.

Summary

- YES is an election system that deals with points to be divided to preferred candidates within the political arena. Therefore more than 1 candidate can be selected as a potential representative for the government. This can be seen in analogy with the boardroom of huge organizations. Because of a more premature participation of younger individuals in our society we become a more generation transcending representation of the government. Candidates are selected based upon their merits and do no need to have a relationship with any political party anymore.
- This system provides the possibility for the voters to make a broader selection of candidates during the election that they can identify with. Individuals to whom their votes are entrusted. Because of the absence of political parties decisions are faster to be made. It is easier to exchange incapable governors because the system is dynamic and it allows doing so by interim referenda about critical issues and their decision makers. Although it is possible to maintain the election period of 4 years actually it is unnecessary because the system is dynamic and keeps on flowing by its flexibility and the possibilities for quick interventions by miscommunication or misbehaviours. However, that won't happen because the intrinsic principles of the system prevent that.
- The modern technology allows creating a flexible and quick interrupting influence by the voters established by digital equipment. The essences of critical themes and their issues in our society don't really change and so the right approach doesn't. Nowadays this approach is the main topic of each debate without truly acknowledging the essences. When capable candidates are in the position to do what the voters ask then it's alright. Otherwise they will immediately be exchanged for capable and integer governors by 1 message of the voter for that moment.

Addition

It may be that you're enthusiastic about YES but you are a little sceptic too. To improve YES we like to go into dialogue with you.
Please sign up the next points for yourself first :

☝ 3 strong aspects of YES

1. --

2. --

3. --

☝ 3 weak aspects of YES

1. --

2. --

3. --

☝ 3 doubtful aspects of YES

1. --

2. --

3. --

If you like to share them with us, send them to:
s.acegr@gmail.com or 2410leonardo@gmail.com

An encore

In fact choosing is about principles and essences. Here you'll find a game to find out about your own preferences. It's called the MaYa-game.

You may play the game in several ways; the ways that helps you understand how YES really functions. First you may take e.g. 10 points and divide all 10 by giving your preferences 1 point. Another method is to take 20 or 30 points and divide all 30, while you are free to give more than 1 point to 1 principle or essence. A restriction may be that you give half the amount to 1 principle or points.

After 2 or 3 months you play the game again. Compare the results of both times with each other and try to find out the "*why*" of your different results.

Table 1

#	Action	Strength	Essence	Points
1	Attracting	Conjoining	Purpose	
2	Stabilizing	Polarizing	Challenge	
3	Connecting	Activating	Service	
4	Measuring	Defining	Form	
5	Evoking	Empowering	Radiation	
6	Balancing	Organizing	Equality	
7	Inspiring	Canalizing	Alignment	
8	Modelling	Harmonizing	Integrity	
9	Realizing	Pulsing	Intention	
10	Producing	Perfecting	Manifestation	
11	Liberating	Solving	Liberation	
12	Universalizing	Dedicating	Cooperation	
13	Transcending	Persisting	Presence	

Table 2

#	Action	Strength	Essence	Points
1	Treasuring	Birth	Being	
2	Communicating	Spirit	Breath	
3	Dreaming	Plenitude	Intuition	
4	Focusing	Flourish	Awareness	
5	Surviving	Vitality	Instinct	
6	Equalizing	Death	Possibility	
7	Knowing	Accomplishment	Healing	
8	Decorating	Elegance	Art	
9	Purifying	Universal-water	Flow	
10	Loving	Heart	Loyalty	
11	Playing	Magic	Illusion	
12	Influencing	Free will	Wisdom	
13	Investigating	Space	Alertness	
14	Enchanting	Timelessness	Openness	
15	Creating	Vision	Spirit	
16	Questioning	Intelligence	Fearlessness	
17	Developing	Navigation	Synchronicity	
18	Reflecting	Endlessness	Order	
19	Catalyzing	Self-generation	Energy	
20	Enlightening	Universal-fire	Life	

System 1 ~ Assign points to every ternary :

- 1 point to your favorites
- Maximally 5 points to assign for table 1
- Maximally 10 points to assign for table 2

System 2 ~ Assign points to every ternary :

- Free number of points to your favorites
- Maximally 10 points to assign for table 1
- Maximally 20 points to assign for table 2
- Maximally half the amount of points per ternary

Table of results ~ single-point system

Date :				
#	**Action**	**Strength**	**Essence**	**Points**
Table 1 ~ first 3 preferences				
Table 2 ~ first 8 preferences				

Table 2 ~ processing ~ count per category/series		
Ternary	**Your choice #**	**Mind priority**
# 1 - 4		In-Put
# 5 - 8		Com-Put ~ Storage
# 9 - 12		Through-Put
# 13 – 16		Out-Put
# 17 - 20		Matrix ~ Life

Table of results ~ pluri-point system

Date :				
#	**Action**	**Strength**	**Essence**	**Points**
Table 1 ~ first 3 preferences				
Table 2 ~ first 8 preferences				

Table 2 ~ processing ~ count per category/series		
Ternary	**Your choice #**	**Mind priority**
# 1 - 4		In-Put
# 5 - 8		Com-Put ~ Storage
# 9 - 12		Through-Put
# 13 - 16		Out-Put
# 17 - 20		Matrix ~ Life

In the last part of the table of results concerning the results of table 2 it shows which of the 5 life processes your own mind prefers. Reflect on the results afterwards; it's the way to know yourself better.

Table 3 & 4

#	Action	Strength	Essence	Points		
1	Treasuring	Birth	Being			
2	Communicating	Spirit	Breath			
3	Dreaming	Plenitude	Intuition			
4	Focusing	Flourish	Awareness			
5	Surviving	Vitality	Instinct			
6	Equalizing	Death	Possibility			
7	Knowing	Accomplishment	Healing			
8	Decorating	Elegance	Art			
9	Purifying	Universal-water	Flow			
10	Loving	Heart	Loyalty			
11	Playing	Magic	Illusion			
12	Influencing	Free will	Wisdom			
13	Investigating	Space	Alertness			
14	Enchanting	Timelessness	Openness			
15	Creating	Vision	Spirit			
16	Questioning	Intelligence	Fearlessness			
17	Developing	Navigation	Synchronicity			
18	Reflecting	Endlessness	Order			
19	Catalyzing	Self-generation	Energy			
20	Enlightening	Universal-fire	Life			

Another fine tuning may be accomplished by fragmenting the ternaries into its elements and assign points at elementary level.

System 3 & 4 ~ Assign points to every element :

- Only 1 point or a free amount of points to your favorites
- Maximally 20 points to assign for table 3 & 4
- Maximally half the amount of points per element
- Maximally (all points / 2) + 1 elements to choose

Table of results ~ single & pluri-point system

Date :				
#	Action	Strength	Essence	Points
Table 3 ~ 1 point per element ~ first 5 preferences				
Table 4 ~ free points per element ~ first 5 preferences				

Table 3 ~ processing ~ 1 point per element ~ per series		
Ternary	**Your choice #**	**Mind priority**
# 1 - 4		In-Put
# 5 - 8		Com-Put ~ Storage
# 9 - 12		Through-Put
# 13 – 16		Out-Put
# 17 - 20		Matrix ~ Life
Table 4 ~ processing ~ free points per element ~ per series		
Ternary	**Your choice #**	**Mind priority**
# 1 - 4		In-Put
# 5 - 8		Com-Put ~ Storage
# 9 - 12		Through-Put
# 13 – 16		Out-Put
# 17 - 20		Matrix ~ Life

About the creator & author

S'ace (Cees) de Groot

Indirector of Waternet ~ Amsterdam since 2001

During this function he introduced and conducted the consciousness processes to bring this institution on higher levels of internal services. His keyword is "*Water*" where water implies an investigating pioneer and the flowing dynamics in life. It implies also the flowing strength of human being. He intends to ensoul or drop the attraction of appreciated naivety.

Besides this in 2007 he was asked by Arun Gandhi ~ grandson of Mahatma Gandhi ~ for being an ambassador of the "*World Unity for Peace Education Department*" ~ related to the Montessori School of Lucknow ~ India. It concerned the international project entitled "*Awakening Planetary Consciousness*". Later in May, 2009 he guided Arun Gandhi during his tour through the Netherlands.

Wil'fred Leonardo Bastiani

PsychoSopher ~ Apprenti since 1971

Since his youth he experienced the values beyond "*Psychosophy*" in an intuitive way. Later he studied all relevant aspects around this discipline and wrote lots of books about it. His keywords are Authenticity, Intelligence, Consciousness and Integrity. Nowadays he is an autonomous and independent investigator concerning Human Nature and only at very special occasions he is willing to be a guest lecturer at universities and relevant institutions about these topics.

www.ingramcontent.com/pod-product-compliance
Ingram Content Group UK Ltd.
Pitfield, Milton Keynes, MK11 3LW, UK
UKHW020228250726
13967UKWH00001B/249

9 781291 695984